MAC'S FIELD GUIDE™

TO ROCKY MOUNTAIN WILDFLOWERS

Habitat :

A –Alpine ridges
D –Disturbed
H –Hillsides
M –Meadows
MW –Wet meadows
P –Sagebrush plains
R –Rocky places
RD –Roadsides/trails
S –Streams/bogs/marshes
W –Woods
WO –Open woods
WR –Rich woods

Evening Primrose
Oenothera caespitosa
A, R; 4"

Sticky Geranium
Geranium viscosissimum
M, S, WO; 20"

Deerhorn Clarkia
Clarkia pulchella
A, D, H; 13"

Fairyslipper
Caypso bulbosa
WR; 6"

Shootingstar
Dodecatheon pauciflorum
M, MW, S; 11"

Twinflower
Linnaea borealis
S, WR; 5"

Canada Thistle
Cirsium arverse
D, M, RD; 42"

Parry Primrose
Primula parryi
M, R, S; 12"

Fireweed
Epilobium angustifolium
D, RD, WO; 60"

Bitteroot
Lewisia rediviva
A, R; 3"

Pink Mountain Heather
Phyllodoce empetriformis
A, MW; 11"

Spotted Knapweed
Centaurea maculosa
D, M, RD; 24"

Long-Leaf Phlox
Phylox longifolia
A, R; 10"

Rosy Pussy Toes
Antennaria rosea
MW, P, R; 7"

Red Monkeyflower
Mimulus lewisii
M, S; 21"

Prince's Pine
Chimaphila umbellata
S, WO; 11"

Pink Wintergreen
Pyrola asarifolia
S, WR; 12"

Bighead Clover
Trifolium macrocephalum
MW, R; 8"

Wild Onion
Allium acuminatum
H, P; 8"

Giant Hyssop
Agastache urticifolia
M, P, WO; 28"

Gayfeather
Liatris punctata
H,P,WO; 18"

Plumed Avens
Geum triflorum
P, R; 15"

Parrots-Beak
Pedicularis racemosa
M, W; 14"

Elephanthead
Pedicularis groenlandica
MW, S; 16"

Foothills Bluebell
Mertensia oblongifolia
H, M, P; 20"

Wyoming Paintbrush
Castilleja linariaefolia
P, R, W; 24"

Scarlet Globemallow
Sphaeralcea coccinea
H, P, RD; 8"

Scarlet Gilia
Ipomopsis aggregata
M, R, WO; 24"

Harebell
Campanula rotundifolia
P, R, WO; 14"

Mountain Gentian
Gentiana calycosa
MW, R, S; 12"

Forget-Me-Not
Myosotis alpestris
A, M; 8"

Blue Penstemon
Penstemon cyaneus
A, P, RD; 24"

Sky Pilot
Polemonium visconsum
A, R; 10"

Silky Phacelia
Phacelia sericea
A, R, RD; 11"

Blue Violet
Viola adunca
S, MW, WR; 5"

Lowbush Penstemon
Penstemon fruticosus
A, P, R; 10"

Tiny Trumpet
Collomia linearis
M; 12"

Monkshood
Aconitum columbianum
MR, MW, S; 45"

Larkspur
Delphinium nuttallianum
A, P, R; 8"

Rocky Mountain Iris
Iris missouriensis
MW; 20"

Bluebonnet
Lupinus sericeus
A, M; 18"

Thickstem Aster
Aster integrifolius
M, WO; 24"

Parry Townsendia
Townsendia parryi
A, H, P; 7"

Pasque Flower
Anemone patens
MW, W; 9"

Clematis
Clematis columbiana
W; varies

Blue Columbine
Aquilegia caerulea
R, WO, WR; 17"

MAC'S FIELD GUIDE™

TO ROCKY MOUNTAIN WILDFLOWERS

The Mountaineers, 1001 SW Klickitat Way, Suite 201, Seattle, WA 98134; (206) 223-6303

Sego Lily
Calochortus nuttallii
A, P, R; 14"

Rocky Mountain Phlox
Phlox multiflora
A, R, WO; 6"

Field Chickweed
Cerastium arvense
A, P, R; 8"

Woodland-Star
Lithophragma parviflora
A, P, WO; 12"

Queen Cup
Clintonia uniflora
S, WR; 6"

Wake-Robin
Trillium ovatum
B, WR; 10"

Alpine Sandwort
Arenaria obtusiloba
A, R; 2"

Marsh Marigold
Caltha leptosepala
M, MW, S; 9"

Wild Strawberry
Fragaria virginiana
M, WO; varies

Cutleaf Daisy
Erigeron compositus
P, R; 6"

Great White Aster
Aster engelmannii
M, WO; 48"

White Bog Orchid
Habenaria dilatata
MW, S, WR; 30"

Star-Flowered Solomon's Seed
Smilacina stellata
M, S, WR; 18"

Pearly Everlasting
Anaphalis margaritacea
D, RD, WO; 24"

Common Yarrow
Achillea lanulosa
A, M, P; 24"

Diamondleaf Saxifrage
Saxifraga rhomboidea
A, P, R; 6"

Beargrass
Xerophyllum tenax
M, W, WO; 36"

White False Hellebore
Veratrum californicum
MW, S; 60"

Valerian
Valerian dioica
MW, R, WO; 14"

Meadow Goldenrod
Solidago canadensis
M, RD, WO; 33"

Yellow Buckwheat
Eriogonum flavum
A, R; 8"

Cow Parsnip
Heracleum lanatum
M, S, WR; 72"

Mountain Buttercup
Ranunculus adoneus
A, M, R; 8"

Mountain False Lupine
Thermopsis montana
H, M; 30"

Dogtooth Violet
Erythronium grandiflorum
P, R, WO; 9"

Spotted Coralroot
Corallorhiza maculata
WR; 18"

Stonecrop
Sedum stenopetalum
R; 6"

Yellow Bell
Fritillaria pudica
H, P; 6"

Alpine Avens
Geum rossii
A, M; 10"

Yellow Monkeyflower
Mimulus guttatus
MW, S; 14"

Bracted Lousewort
Pedicularis bracteosa
MW, WR; 24"

Ivesia
Ivesia gordonii
A, M, R; 5"

Cinquefoil
Potentilla gracilis
MW, S, WR; 18"

Blanketflower
Gaillardia aristata
D, M, RD; 18"

Western Wallflower
Erysimum asperum
H, P; 21"

Western Yellow Violet
Viola nuttallii
P, W; 2"

Groundsel
Senecio integerrimus
P, W; 18"

Alpine Sunflower
Hymenoxys grandiflora
A, R; 12"

Blazing Star
Mentzelia laevicaulis
D, P, RD; 36"

Balsamroot
Balsamorhiza sagitatta
H, P, R; 15"

Goldeneye
Viguiera multiflora
H, M; 30"

Illustrations by David Sauskojus

50495
9 780898 863369
ISBN 0-89886-336-8